INFRASTRUCTURE

Also by Jerry Martien

Rocks Along the Coast
(Poetry Chapbook, 1984)

Sky Over Taylor Peak
(Poetry Chapbook, 1987)

Journey Work
(Poetry Chapbook, 1989)

*Shell Game:
A True Account of Beads and Money in North America*
(Nonfiction, 1996)

Pieces in Place
(Poetry Collection, 1999)

*The Price of a Life:
Shell, Gold, Carbon Notes & Weed. Four Kinds of Money
in the Humboldt Bay / Six Rivers Region*
(Nonfiction, 2016)

Earth Tickets
(Poetry Collection, 2017)

Before the Flood
(Poetry Chapbook, 2017)

INFRASTRUCTURE

DREAMS, DIVINATIONS & DISPATCHES
FROM THE UNDERGROUND

JERRY MARTIEN

Many Names Press
Blue Lake, California

Copyright © by Jerry Martien

All rights reserved. No part of this book may be reproduced, stored in a retrieval system, or transmitted in any form, by any means electronic, mechanical, photocopied, recorded or otherwise, except when using "fair use" quotes embodied in articles or reviews, and not-for-profit educational growth purposes.

Many Names Press Edition, October, 2022.
ISBN: 978-1-944497-06-4
Library of Congress Control Number: 2022946849

Kate Hitt, Many Names Press
khitt@ManyNamesPress.com
+1-831-728-4302

Jerry Martien   JerryMartien@gmail.com

Cover Design by Annie Reid, www.AnnieReid.com

Note to Accompany the Second Edition

Infrastructure was originally designed and published in 2020 in a limited edition of 250 copies by Bug Press in Arcata, California, and underwritten by subscription.

This edition by Many Names Press is distributed and available worldwide through Ingram and Amazon. Please support the environment and reduce the carbon footprint by buying books at your local independent bookstore, which can be found at Indiebound.org. Special discounts are available for bulk purchase by contacting the publisher or author.

*To the Underground
& All Who There Abide*

Acknowledgments

Thanks to Jenny Finch, reader, listener, and companion on many of these journeys.

Thank you, Annie Reid, for the cover I had long imagined. To Kathy Glass, for the mistakes you'll never see. To Robert Arena and the crew at Bug Press, for the labor that first saw this book into the world as a limited edition. And to Kate Hitt and her Many Names Press, for the many hours of care invested in producing and publishing this edition.

My deep appreciation and thanks to the H.J. Andrews Forest Blue River Writers gatherings, and for a writing residence where portions of this book began. And for Playa at Summer Lake's artists in residence program, where it assumed its present form.

A grateful acknowledgment to the editors and publishers who made a place for:
"Design" in The H.J. Andrews' *The Forest Log*, and in *Forest Under Story: Creative Inquiry in an Old Growth Forest* (U.WA. 2016) ed. Brodie, Goodrich, & Swanson; "I Dreamed I Was at a Watershed Meeting" in North Coast Environmental Center's *Econews* (2012) and Planet Drum Foundation's *Pulse* (2014); "Infrastructure" in the Island Institute's journal, *Connotations* (Spring 2014); "July in Eureka" in *North Coast Journal* (July 16–22, 2009); "Looking Upstream" letterpress broadside by Jerry Reddan, Tangram Press (Berkeley, 2015); "Return of the Dead Log People" in *The Forest Log* and in *Rot: The Afterlife of Trees*, a catalog of multi-media presentations, Corvallis Arts Center, Jan.-Feb. 2016; "Second Lives" in Vol. I / Issue 1 of *The Sextant Review* (2019); "Small, Feathered Consolations" via Dan Brewer's *Mail a Poem* (2015); and "To a Northern Spotted Owl" in *Make It True: Poetry from Cascadia*, ed. Paul Nelson et al. (2015).

CONTENTS

I. SOMEBODY STARTS TALKING

Beginning with A	1
Design	2
Maintenance	4
Refuge	7
The Powder Post Beetle	9
My Life with Mickey Mouse	10
Graduation	12

II. ANOTHER DAY IN PARADISE

They Start a New Garden	17
Composition for Upright Piano & 1988 Toyota Camry	18
Putting Up the Tent	23
As If They Had No Place to Talk But in the Dreams of the Living	24
July in Eureka	25
After the Crash	26

III. NINE DAYS OUT

Day One. They Arrive from the Underworld	31
Day Two. They Pray for Change	33
Day Three. In the Devil's Kitchen	35
Day Four. Advice from the Devil	37
Day Five. Viewing the Wild Life	39
Day Six. Where the West Began	41
Day Seven. Snowballs in Hell	43
Day Eight. Filling the Emptiness	45
Day Nine. They Pause before Returning	47

IV. IT ALL COMES BACK

 Second Lives   53
 return of the dead log people   56
 Dear Sue   58
 The Monument   60
 Shopping for the Revolution   64
 Unwrapping the Sun   67

V. KEEPING OUR DARKNESS

 east bay dream with power lines   71
 geology of the eastern sierra   73
 A Walk with Federico García Lorca   77
 I Dreamed I Was at a Watershed Meeting   82
 Infrastructure   83
 Small, Feathered Consolations   88
 To a Northern Spotted Owl   89

VI. LEAVING THE LIGHTS ON

 Exhibit Ahead   95
 Understanding Capitalism   98
 The Wall   101
 Blue Star   104
 Home Improvement   106
 The Way and the Light   108
 looking upstream   111

NOTES   113
ABOUT THE AUTHOR   121
COLOPHON   123

I. SOMEBODY STARTS TALKING

Beginning with A

Somebody starts talking but it's not me. It's a woman's voice. She only starts talking when I stop. Shut up, she says. Listen. When I start inventing things to say, she stops. Nothing. Nobody there. *Callete la boca*, the first sentence I learned in Spanish. Shut up. I was told: *Speak English*. A silence where another language had been.

Listen. It's Saturday morning. November. From across the fields the muffled echo of a shotgun. Blam, says the voice. A dead duck goes into the poem. Next door the neighbor already drunk and on her pain meds is calling Here kitty. Here, kitty kitty. When I call our cat he runs the other way. Here, muse. The poem stops.

Silence is muse to the word that comes unbidden. The neighbor is still calling kitty kitty but in a higher voice. Maybe her cat ran away with our cat. Here, poem. Hear poem. Hear the words of my calling.

My first-grade teacher was so beautiful I didn't tell her I could already read. Miss Aaron would sit on the curb outside the classroom at lunch time and let me practice reading aloud. She ate her sandwich from a paper sack the same as mine. She wore a red dress and red lipstick and wore her long brown hair swept up and braided.

Sometimes Miss Aaron would get a letter from a soldier fighting somewhere in the Pacific and read it to herself. Her blue eyes looking into places beyond words. That's why I joined up. It was long ago and far away but she can still hear me. She loves the way I fight to save language and meaning. Her blue eyes listen. Sunlight reflects from her hair. I stop reading. Her red mouth opens and the words come.

Design

Three old poets standing on a wooden bridge in the forest. Clem admires its pole construction, the craftily fitted joints. Made in a shop, Charles says. Brought here and assembled. Lookout Creek rushing beneath us.

The trail winds among massive trunks of old-growth Douglas fir. Standing and fallen. Decomposing into duff. Spared the clear-cuts of the surrounding mountains, here the millions of years go on. *Refugia*, Charles says. Places where life goes on.

He bends down and picks up a big leaf of prehistoric lettuce. Hands me a piece. *Lobaria*, he says. Ancient lichen, hollows and ridges like the landscape of another world. Now I see it up in the canopy, scattered on the forest floor. Green and gray. Thriving and dying. He hands a piece to Clem, describes how it works.

A fungus and an algae hooked up with a bacterium. It can photosynthesize, reproduce from spores or broken pieces of itself. Takes nitrogen from the air, gives it to the trees. How the forest goes on.

Clem stops beside a small yew. Wraps his hand around a centuries-old branch. The English long-bow, he says. Battle of Agincourt. Henry V? He laughs at the French generals whining about rules of war. Clem admires a good tool.

Then, Devil's Club, Charles says. Pointing at spiny stalks thrust up through the forest floor. With wrapped burlap for a hand-hold, he says, company goons beat the Wobblies when they ran them out of Everett and other mill towns. I touch one, spines sharp as needles. Ingenious, I say. A moment of silence for the IWW.

At a wide spot in the trail, three old poets looking up at a spider's web. Strung between yews on either side, an artful airy construct, its author in the middle of it.

Pollen from the fir trees has dusted the spider and every strut and strand with gold. All that beauty. Useless, now that it's visible.
Poor guy, we agree.
He'll never get dinner with that.

Maintenance

Rusty and bullet-holed sheets of corrugated tin enclose the pool and a narrow room where we undress. The walls and roof shield us from wind and the unpaved highway along the edge of the playa. On a long wooden bench in the dressing room, initials and names are carved beside the names of who they love. On one wall, on plywood screwed into weathered 2x4s, a black and white photo. And a typed inscription:

> *In memory of Carl.*
> *You touched many lives*
> *and you will be missed.*

In the photo a lean and bent-shouldered man in overalls looks up from an opening in the tin walls. The concrete pool is empty. He's smiling, holding a shovel.

From the dressing room we walk along a weathered deck, step through the opening, descend a wooden ladder into the hot water, the dark and heavy air.

After a while I move to an adjoining pool, a little cooler and open to the overarching blue. Jenny is lying on a towel on the deck. On the eastern horizon, across the dry lake, mountains of rose-black and rose-blue. To the west, above the road, Steens Mountain rising and rising. White jagged traces of snow in July.

From the bank below the road, heated by whatever has pushed that thirty miles of rock into the sky, a steaming alluvial fan weaves into a single stream. A pipe brings it into the bath, it spills over, meanders into the sagebrush and disappears.
Most of the bath house materials are salvaged or found. Like Carl's labor, a gift from the local community. A boon to

weary travelers. We come down each morning from our campsite a couple of miles up the mountain.

To imagine and build this bath house was a holy act. It's a temple to our oldest gods. The air smells of sulfur. In the steaming rivulets flowing from beneath the mountain, unearthly molds of orange and green and black. The bottom of the pool is dark and slippery.

But the holiest act, the gift without price, is to clean and renew the temple. To keep scraping out the muck, as Carl is doing in the photo. As others will do now, who put the photo on the wall. Priceless, because the mold never sleeps and will ultimately defeat every effort to suppress and remove it. Because, as Jenny said as we walked from the road and stopped to wonder at the unearthly colors, it's whence we came.

From a place that doesn't care about community and our naked conviviality. That eats even concrete and leaves its slime on everything mortal and dear. An old man in dirty overalls parks his pickup and walks down from the road. Slack-jawed, wordless, he sits on a bench and stares. When I ask him if he's waiting to bathe he gets up and walks back to the highway. Trash is scattered along the path. Bullet holes in everything an eye can aim at. Carl's photo has been slashed with a knife.

Human nature, given a little love and a shovel, can redeem and cleanse itself. We carry out empty beer cans. Repair the wire gate by the highway. Say thank you to the water and whence it came.

And to Carl:

*May you now and always
beneath Steens Mountain
bathe with the gods*

Refuge (Occupy Humboldt 2012)

When I was a child the Jews of Europe were in hiding. Along with gypsies, commies, queers, dissidents—anyone who wasn't a good fascist. A few brave people gave them shelter. Hid them in forests. Caves. Sewers. And secret rooms in their homes.

A guy with a tool box would show up at your door. Good morning. I'm a carpenter with the resistance. Show me around your house. I'll make a hiding place. A secret door. Maybe a way out the back.

When I grew up I worked as a carpenter, often in the homes of dissidents. I hung doors opening into divergent spaces. Installed windows with alternative views. But it was after the war. My work didn't have to be concealed. The job should have been easy.

But the fascists don't really go away. They change uniforms, make new promises of security. They come at night—to prevent terror, they say. They come in the morning—to relocate us, for our safety, they say. They appear on TV. Evacuate, they declare. The levee. The reactor. The social plan. Has failed. They watch us, question us, pay concrete workers and lawyers to build rooms with no way out.

Now I'm too old to carpenter. Work with words instead of lumber. All the doors are in plain sight. Transparency my last and only refuge. This house is what it plainly says. Even a fascist can get it. The foundations and walls are a few old words. Amendments to the words. Come in, people say. You must be from the resistance.

I step inside. The place is bigger than it looks. My work is off in one corner. But there will be rooms for everyone. This entire town and its history of removals. The Wiyot. Chinese. Wobblies. The hapless, homeless, and undocumented. People deprived of liberty or livelihood because they threaten that perfect marriage of money and guns that is the essence of fascism.

For a fall and a winter this room was our house of government. In plain sight on its concrete steps, on its sidewalk and street, on the grass the cops built a fence around. It was visible in the signs people hung on the fence. On the faces of people arrested when the cops took the signs down.

There's a lot to do. I set down my tools. Start making a plan.

The Powder Post Beetle

He's a model revolutionary.
Burrows from within.
Works quietly. Troubles no one.
The home inspector describes him:
small, helpless, easily crushed between the fingers.
But we don't find him, only his handiwork.
The inspector brings out a handful of sub-floor.
Fragments of papery wood. And powder, of course.
A note saying, So long and thanks.

I tear out the threshold, sister new joists
under the old fir flooring, the tiny holes
I've lived with for nearly twenty years.
The holes will be sprayed, the new owners
untroubled by threats of subversion.
I've heard they only come out of their holes
to make love—but like us, maybe they
also wanted a sunnier location.

The note left no forwarding address.

My Life with Mickey Mouse

I was a posthumous kid. Mother was a flapper from San Berdoo. Father was from Bialystok, did wardrobe for 20th Century Fox. Like most of the grownups they died in the war. I was raised by a crazy aunt who lived in a little yellow house in the middle of an orange grove in Anaheim.

In spring we had to cover our ears and stay in the house the bees were so loud. The blossoms that sweet. In the early '50s men came with tractors and cranes and pulled up all the orange trees and burned them and they built Disneyland next door.

Mickey Mouse was our neighbor. I would wave at Goofy in the morning on the way to school. I don't think my aunt noticed the change in the neighborhood. She worked as a riveter at Douglas during the War and then she was a maid at the Pickwick till they tore it down.

She was working as a telephone operator the day I got home from high school just as the phone rang. She said, "Jerry, you're on your own. I've worked myself to death." The line went silent. Then: "Look in the freezer."

I lived in the house till the end of my senior year. Each month I'd take a few dollars from the Tupperware box at the back of the freezer. That summer I took out the last bill. Under it was a folded paper, some kind of map. I was reading it when there was a knock at the door. It was Mickey.

"You'll have to move," he said. "We bought this house and we're tearing it down. Business is good." He smiled and waved his white-gloved hand. Then he walked back next door to Disneyland.

The map showed the way to a lost gold mine somewhere in the San Bernardino mountains. My aunt had talked about it for years, whenever she was going crazy. I threw away the map and sat down to write Mickey Mouse a letter.

I wasn't going to move. Like, this was my home, right?

Graduation

When we come out at Sather Gate I know where I am again. From BART we had walked up to campus, followed a concrete promenade across the green lawn and through a grove of oak. Somewhere underneath us Strawberry Creek. Along the walkway, suspended from light poles, large banners with blown-up photos of UC Berkeley students.

Lindsay points to the guy she and her friends think is the cutest. Some of them will be freshmen here next fall. She's going south to UCLA. Like her sister she sees directions I could not have imagined.

I recognize the auditorium where I took them to hear Dylan a couple of years ago. Julia puts her hands over her ears. O my god, she says. That was so loud.

We're going to buy graduation presents. Posters. Something they know I can afford. One for the bare walls of a freshman dorm room, one for walls filled with icons of East Bay twenty-first-century teenage lives.

Whatever is happening to time is also changing space. I think Telegraph is the other way and lead us two blocks in the wrong direction. We wondered where you were going.

Following them along the bead and incense Hare Krishna avenue I slip back half a century, their grandmother and I stopping here overnight on the way to another life. Out of the southern California hills, along these tree-shaded streets, shingled houses and cultured quiet about to change forever.

Next morning I dropped off my last undergraduate writing

before we headed north and east. '53 Mercury sedan, U-Haul trailer, a year-old child in the back. On our way to a world we thought must be out there.

On our way to school, looking for things that school can't teach. How to listen to our hearts. Calling us out. Calling us back.

The poster shop on Telegraph is still there. For an hour we look through images of the past few hundred years until they each find a small poster. Then we walk back another way, stop at a little cafe for some kind of frozen dessert.

Out the window I see the white Mercury 4-door and the orange trailer rumbling along the avenue and through the quiet streets. Your father, I tell them, was asleep on the back seat. We were lost.

The heart in its wisdom calls us. Foresees these bright spirits and sends them to guide us.

II. ANOTHER DAY IN PARADISE

They Start a New Garden

It's a hot and hungry new planet.

A quarter billion of their kind driven from the garden. He's lucky to have a shovel and a place to dig.

He stops to rest in the shade of the new-leafed apple. Drinks from a glass of mineral water chilled by the PG&E plant just over the hill. Fires burning day and night.

With the cedars of Oregon he has built a wall around a pile of earth. A raised bed like they had in Eden.

From the compost box he brought worms, their intimacy with offal and rot. Some day his own used-up remains. He loves the way they take it all in. Coming out clean.

He turned them gently into the soil, recited prayers and derivations. Wyrm, the ancient dragon, suppressed and denied by a nation so clean and godly that even Death doesn't want to touch it. He's re-introducing the serpent to the garden.

He also invited a gopher who ate half a row of carrots before the trap finally got him.

Now he's built a subterranean wall of half-inch rabbit wire. All he has to do is fill the trench back in.

Eve worries he's going to drop dead out there. All their money gone for lumber and soil amendment. They'll have to borrow for seed.

The gopher's coat was a glossy chestnut brown. Maybe they should forget carrots, raise gophers instead. Or go back to the hunting and gathering.

He tries to remember all the gardens they've started. Earth turned over and over. The garden becoming the farm. The trouble they're in.

He gets up from the green ground, the fading blossoms. Puts on hat and gloves and sunglasses. Picks up the shovel. Begs again the earth's forgiveness.

Composition for Upright Piano & 1988 Toyota Camry

> *When you're playing with musicians who think this way you can do anything. Anybody can stop and let the others go on.*
> —Charles Mingus

The music is coming from an old ranch house in the Sonoma hills. On the missing keys of an ancient piano someone is playing a tune just at the edge of our range of hearing. Or beyond for those who listened too long when the music was loud.

Not all of us are hearing or not hearing the same tune. Not all of us having the same memory or perception of the space through which time has passed and is passing now. The music being made visible by images that change with the tempo of its not quite heard notes.

Like yesterday the green Forester on the dusty mid-summer road changing to a thirty-five-years-ago maroon VW bus slipping and sliding over a mud-tracked meadow in the October rain. The children then in line to be born now elders to the young ones who are themselves no longer children. So then who is left? Sudden death and slow has taken several of us and many fine old tan oaks. This changes the music.

The only exception—the counterpoint—is little Iris who is just at the use-your-words stage. Where we've all been at one time or another and some of us recently again. In this way the composition does not change at all.

The music rises from the motion of the planet in relation to the sun moon and stars and operates by means of gears and ratchets and electro-magnetism. Music of the spheres it's been called but its real source is this piano in the old ranch house at the end of a dirt road in the Sonoma hills. It's been playing since the beginning of time and is so far out of tune it can't be heard except maybe by some of the dogs. It can be reproduced on almost anything mechanical as long as it's properly grounded. An old car in this case.

The composition in its second movement calls for a tow chain, a 4WD pickup, and a red Toyota sedan with weeds growing around it. With a human chorus of past and present voices. And of course the dogs. One in the pickup, let it be a retriever. A dachshund will work for the Toyota's passenger seat. And one of those black and white cow dogs in the back to keep an eye on the driver. Any licensed or unlicensed being may get behind the wheel of either vehicle.

Now we tow the car out of the driveway and onto the road.

Chorus, please. Okay, now jump the battery. Turn it over. Give it the gas. Blooey. A rat's nest and two acorns blow out of the tail pipe. Hallelujahs from the chorus, thank you. The windshield is washed. The formerly blind claim they can see. Everyone eats guacamole and votes for their favorite, and the usual hard core stays up playing poker through the shortest night of the year.

The third movement is enacted the following day. Summer solstice for those using their words. It requires the actual piano that has kept the universe going all these years plus another larger and older pickup which need not be street legal, only running. And the chorus and several engineers, dozens of grips and extras, and of course the animal wranglers.

But first everyone has to be fed again, after which the votes are counted in the guacamole run-off and democracy is restored. Then the family theme is reintroduced by a duet of contested ownership: It's your old piano. No, mother, it's your old piano. Then there's the backing of the pickup up the driveway followed by the choreographed removal of two doors of the house. Making way at last for the fourth and so far only real movement in which the piano is literally lifted by six to eight extras and carried ten steps. The sun stops in the sky.

Again: lifted by six to eight extras and carried ten steps. Each time the piano rests someone who once had piano lessons must affirm that it's beyond tuning by performing passages of spontaneous atonal composition with particular stress on the silent or only vaguely percussive keys. Thunk-silence-thunk. Thunk-a-thunk.

The pause for the marking of musical time affords the advocates of brute force an opportunity to challenge the engineers and demonstrate tools and methods long considered obsolete or lost. Lengths of 2x4 are employed despite the warnings, advice, and ridicule of those who first advanced this project. A sub-chorus of hecklers and nay-sayers insist we will all be spun off the earth. Others demand a full environmental review. Some want a recount of the guacamole vote.

Once the piano turns the corner from the kitchen onto the porch now reinforced by ¾ inch plywood, the pickup must be backed and forwarded seven times to be sure it doesn't scrape the top step due to settling of the springs when the piano hits the bed. Thunk thunk.

From there the fifth and final movement is basically a promenade of three or four generations each to its own tune dancing alongside the truck or hanging from its bed and out its passenger window accompanied by the discordant notes of the rabble along the dirt road in amazement laughing or lamenting as the procession goes on with the piano now playing itself.

Little Iris wakes up from her nap and claps her hands and the sun begins to move again.

Now the piano remembers every tune it has ever played as it is carried through the grove of remaining tan oak and madrone and out onto the open ridge where the road ends and the piano goes on.

Playing for another year for the living and the dead and a few curious cows the unceasing tune of the sun and moon and stars to the accompaniment of barking dogs and all the music that lives in human memory.

Cazadero,
Summer 2009

Putting Up the Tent

Epithalamion for Aryay and Marcia

They've come here to find peace together.
A wooded valley. Mountains north and south.
A lake higher up, a stream flowing through.
Each with a picture of where they are.
Where the tent should go.
Which direction its door will face.
Where sun and shade will fall.
Which way their bed will lie.
Is the ground smooth. Is it dry.
Too far in the woods. Too near the creek.
Will they be safe from bears.
Who will inflate the ThermaRest.
Where the cooking should be done.
Who'll set up the stove.
Some decisions are hers. Some are his.
They have words. Act on them.
Put up the tent. Go their separate ways.
He sits by the creek. She walks to the lake.
The mountains watch them. Say nothing.
A pair of ravens near the creek
laugh and cry and scold. Fly together
to a branch of an old cottonwood.
Intimate gestures. Foolish noises.
Ravens. Mountains. Lake and stream.
Man and woman. They're all in the tent.
The tent is their world. Their wedding.
Wish them peace together.

As If They Had No Place to Talk
But in the Dreams of the Living

We were at one of those underground parties we used to have around here and sometime after midnight Wyn decided we should drive to the City in his gray panel truck, the one our friend John later shot himself in. Wyn could be excruciatingly deliberate and slow even when he was alive but this night we got off to a good start and were cruising southward about an hour or two into the small hours when we stopped at this Extinct Wildlife Park. A busload of tourists had also stopped, visiting Humboldt County from the underworld. And there to our surprise was Bob Dodge among the crowd and he and Wyn started yakking non-stop about the weather and the quality of this year's weed and on and on so I couldn't get a word in edgewise till finally I just started talking too while they carried on in what might as well have been a foreign language, not caring in the least what sense it made or what time of Earth's night or day it might be or whether we'd ever get to the goddam City at all. As if gathering enough breath to finish the next sentence was the only thing on Earth that really mattered.

July in Eureka

for Paula

About a dozen people seated on folding chairs in the rotunda of the Morris Graves Museum. The old brick building at Sixth and F that used to be the library. It's Sunday afternoon free jazz. A four-piece combo backing up a singer: *April in Paris*.

The town is hushed and gray. Its citizens have fled to the hills or are hiding indoors. The singer's voice an island in the fog.

I've known her through several lives. In one she was married to a fisherman who was lost at sea. Over the years we've met and talked, often at public meetings where she's always spoken on behalf of good causes. Now she's a jazz singer.

I keep taking off and putting back on my sunglasses. Coming in from a side window, something not exactly bright but blinding. A watery ghost of sunlight.

When she finishes we applaud and a kid with a saxophone comes up. He's good but needs a few more summers in him. I listen as I walk into the gallery and sit down in front of Morris's heron triptych.

Imagined lives. Former lives. This gray afternoon.

> The music flows down F Street to the bay
>   finds a vessel tied at the dock.
> Heads out toward the bar and the open sea
>   without waiting for the fog to clear.

After the Crash

Demolition Derby Night, Modoc County Fair

It's a perfect summer evening for destruction. The cows and the cowboys have had their fun. Everyone's been stuffed with barbecue and hot dogs and tilt-a-whirled. The beer is flowing. The stadium is packed. The fire department is standing by with two trucks and an ambulance. The water truck has soaked the arena so the cars can't get quite enough traction to actually kill anybody.

One by one to cheers and applause they come spinning and careening onto the field. Fire blasts and roars straight up from the engines so the drivers can hardly see where they're going and no one can hear a thing. Mud is thrown in all directions. The crowd loves it. At last all sixteen cars are in place. People and machines rarin' to go. When the announcer asks for applause, he gets it.

In the black and green '78 Fairlane wagon. Number 87. Johnny Darkness.

Hoorah. Go, Johnny.

Number 13. Amanda Trueheart. In her maroon '76 Mercury Marquis.

Yay, Amanda. We love you.

The loudest applause goes to a pair of late-model white Chevys put up by the Save-the-Hospital campaign. All the nation's money is gone into the crusades and offshore accounts so its remote little towns try to raise a few dollars with carnival rides and cotton candy and if they're lucky a little wreckage they can live with.

It's a ritual sacrifice of the things for which Americans sacrifice every day without acknowledgment or recompense. Oil. Steel. Empire. A world on fire. Smoke and flames and sirens going off. Wait. Sirens going off. A car's on fire. For a moment the crashing and smashing stops. Fire trucks rush onto the field. They douse the flames. The car still runs. The crowd goes wild. Then the destruction resumes.

Now the loudest applause is for the biggest crash. The one from all the way across the arena that rips off half a car. Everyone yells for Johnny. Amanda is loved more than ever. The Save-the-Hospital cars are torn to pieces. The crowd doesn't care. Johnny wins. Amanda wins. Half the people in the crowd win something in the intermission drawing. A night at the spa. A case of motor oil. A manicure. Twenty-five dollars' worth of groceries. The thousand-dollar grand prize is divided among the survivors.

It was better than the Iraq War. No one died. Admission was only eight dollars. When we get down to the last real cars and the last barrel of oil
        this is how we'll burn it.

III. NINE DAYS OUT

day one.
they arrive from the underworld

    those who live below
    the people we
    think we know

    also have their
    issues
    shitty jobs
    bills to pay

    (only in heaven
    do we live forever
    on credit)

    & like us they
    need to escape
    the little hells
    their lives become

    they pump up
    fossil ooze
    pave their way
    with its darkness

    refine & burn it
    in phlegythonic engines
    & thus transport themselves
    to where the pavement ends
    or the ooze runs out

    they want to get burned
    by a real star

look into
instead of out of
their cratered love

stew in someone
else's cauldron

seeking change
lost in dark
stygian pilgrims

read directions
written in the dark

take a wrong turn
camp in a bog

eat in darkness
eaten by things unseen

wake up on earth
sunshine
        coffee
                skunk cabbage

home can be
any place but home

Mill Creek

day two.
they pray for change

>he's afraid of heights
>she worries about
>getting in too deep
>
>a hopeless agoraphobe
>a claustrophobic mess
>
>the way to the volcano
>blocked by snow
>
>a western marmot
>with a sign
>mountain closed
>
>no ranger to interpret
>those bright red erections—
>*snow* plant?
>
>the underground
>already here
>
>persephone
>on spring break
>
>their idea of
>where they're from
>downwardly revised
>
>was not papa lightning
>in mama's soup
>
>was her hot mineral

upwelling
bubbles in a spermy sea

bottom up instead of
top down over-
turns overturning

reveals us as
self-motating hyper-heated
babbling slime mold

ancient shoreline
high on the mountain

pyroclastic boulder
blasted (1915!)
fifty miles away

they set up camp
far down the volcano

he likes it in the trees
she prefers the blast zone

black coffee with
evening prayer

o mama
somebody's rewriting
the book of changes

in the tent in the dark
age upon age overturning

Mt. Lassen

**day three.
in the devil's kitchen**

> *...for going out, I found, was really going in.*
> —John Muir

angels of the underworld

think our hot spring
is niagara falls

our hissing fumarole
champagne

bubbling mud pot
honeymoon dinner

our chili
beans and rice

their rice and beans
and chili again?

one too many likeness

the cook walks
to a snow-melt stream
dips her fingers
near a steaming vent
too hot to touch

try it, she says

fire   ice
nothing between

water from heaven
meet water from hell

the cook returns
with the earth & sky

feeds the body
   feeds the soul

my tortilla
       your tortilla

Mt. Lassen

day four.
advice from the devil

    painter   potter
    bird bone player
    house wife   well digger
    candidate for ufo abduction

    souls uneasy
    in the dreamless fields
    of anthropocene america

    they come here
    refugees from love

    on the edge
    of a wide & empty valley
    camp set up
    chili steaming

    up the road a
    cloud of dust
    her ex in 4-wheel drive

    he stops
    unfolds a map

    follow it he says
    but give it back

    they give it back

    look out he says for
    drunk off-roaders
    spot lights

shots in the dark

by day beware
flash flood
roads that turn
to mud

& o yeah
rattlesnakes

he admires their sun shade

as soon as he leaves
the wind blows it down

next morning
a cloud of dust
stops
         backs up

one more thing he says
dust

& as soon as he leaves
it rains

Surprise Valley

**day five.
viewing the wild life**

    tourists from deep space
    miss earth
    land on planet x

    find its underworld
    still in place

    gods that
    still talk to strangers

    do you think we
    made all this herb
    & herbivore
    just for you to rope &
    brand & sing about?

    to save the unknown
    following the known
    agencies revise
    management priorities

    tag & collar &
    count it all instead

    seeking things to
    eye-dee
    pilgrims sing home
    home on the
    picnic in the wind & sage

    & the gods send
    off rhyme and ant

not antelope

1000s of acres of forb
100 miles of dirt road
dedicated signage
wildlife viewing opportunity

back in camp
a zero on their life list
                    but look—

the buffalo may roam
mostly in hell

& deer mostly play
in its suburbs

but the antelope
graze alfalfa
in a nearby field

seeking answers
they forgot the question

Sheldon Antelope Preserve

day six.
where the west began

> *One cannot get rid of anything,*
> *one cannot get over anything,*
> *one cannot repel anything—everything hurts.*
> —Friedrich Nietzsche

o you
pioneers

to our planet's
surface

wouldn't this make a
great desert?

you put up signs

carve from
rock & white space
private afterlives
& around them string
the bob-wire
of bad dreams

you institutionalize
the fear of losing
what was never yours

obscure the horizon
with false instruction

win
big

*cheap
divorce*

sole & despotic dominion

just keep moving
as if you understand it

sports wagon going west
head-ons station wagon
on its way back east

more of the same or bust

sagebrush
            alkali
                      rock

to own any piece of it
you have to own it all

day seven.
snowballs in hell

>they get the call
>get outa town
>
>go to nevada
>chill
>
>escape the heat
>leap from the frying pan
>
>drive from town to
>desert town
>begging with a 40-quart cooler
>
>go 50 miles for ice cream
>
>forswear the devils
>of desert religion
>
>the paradise
>of their fathers
>
>the purgatory
>of underground testing
>
>a church that dams
>& diverts rivers
>to absolve its sins
>
>cuts through
>theological knots
>with licensed brothels
>& short odds

the bones of pilgrims
picked clean
of dead meat & dogma
get up from the
side of the road & go on

camp beside cottonwoods
ignore the sign

PRIVATE PROPERTY

under the stars
inside the tent

the laws of your heaven
don't apply

Black Rock Desert

**day eight.
filling the emptiness**

>gas up
>where you can
>buy ice &
>seek direction
>when you must
>
>see where they manufacture
>sheetrock
>to line the walls
>of suburban civilization
>
>rock
>is all there is
>to do out here
>
>mine it make it
>or haul it for the S-P
>
>out of the basin
>on blazing iron rails
>a hundred weeping cars of ore
>
>dragged away by
>throbbing yellow & orange
>diesel gods
>
>along the tracks
>below the grade
>the pilgrims find
>sanctuary

in a bubbling scalding
pool
        whose other end
is otherworldly green
cattails
monster polliwogs
& the mother of mud

the pilgrims' way is
always through the hot end

next morning
3 white citizens
a pickup a trailer a jeep
3 quads & 4 cases
of bud natural

the pilgrims' way now
pick up trash and go

over at the
relocation center
above their tent
half of heaven is
one single mountain

the only way
        across this desert
               is around that rock

Empire / Trego Springs / Calico Mountains

**day nine.
they pause before returning**

> *Words are the only thing that last forever.*
> —Doobie, the Guru of Gerlach

    souls crossing
    crossing again
    the paths of other souls

    the only way
    is to lose the way
    that got them here

    roadside attractions
    picture post cards
    of things not themselves

    out on the desert
    pilgrims seek the real
    names again

    balsamroot
    lupine
    penstemon
    flax

    locoweed
    larkspur
    paintbrush
    & basin rayless daisy

    calico granite black rock
    ranges beyond knowing

sagebrush playa
white space

white space
& time

& a sign saying
stop
turn here
get the real
news from rocks

of people's names
rhymes
jokes
aphorisms
something someone said

pilgrims
on their trip's last leg
stop to read the faded paint

where a desert poet
recorded unrecorded
desert people's
   dates
memories
   promises
(emptiness)

word of heaven
meet word from rock

which pilgrims use
to renew vows
forgive differences
forget likeness

kiss hello
        say goodbye
to the people they
        used to know

pack up whatever is
        left
& back across the desert
        go and go and go

Guru Road, Gerlach Nevada

IV. IT ALL COMES BACK

Second Lives

*That's all we have, finally, the words, and they
had better be the right ones.*
—Raymond Carver

It was one of those old motor inns, on a hill overlooking the Mad River where it widens before emptying into the Pacific. A late '70s summer afternoon. The famous writer was sitting on the bed. He'd invited a bunch of us over from the bar. Poets and writers, the writer who'd been his teacher, friends who lived and drank with writers, who talked like writers when they drank.

He was trying to get sober.

The scene lives in my memory with another room. A long time before, a Sunday when I was fifteen. My step-dad had asked me to take a drive with him over to Corona, to see a cousin of his from Texas who was dying.

Mac hadn't asked me to go anywhere for a while. The last time might have been the weekend we drove to the phone company yard in San Jacinto. He was line foreman again and had a key. We loaded up the trunk of the '49 Ford with lead-wrapped phone cable so he and a buddy could melt it into fishing weights, sell the copper to buy beer.

I wasn't around much for fishing anymore. I was too busy hanging out at the Texaco and smoking cigarettes. Avoiding grownups and their lives.

Grover was the cousin's name. Mac never said what he was dying of. Dressed in shirt and slacks, brown shoes, he sat on the bed in a room in this old hotel in downtown Corona. Mac and I sat in the two chairs. The shades were pulled down.

The motel was at the edge of McKinleyville, a little town of trailer parks with a Safeway and sewage running in the ditches. The Bella Vista Inn. All it had going for it was that view of the river and ocean.

There weren't enough chairs, so a couple of us sat on the bed. He's done for, I thought. Finished as a writer.

Mac and Grover talked about west Texas summers when they were kids. Coming out to California. The war. How different things turned out from what they thought.

Then Mac said to Grover, show him your toes. I wasn't sure I'd heard right, but Grover unlaced one shoe and took the sock off. He had webbed toes. Both feet? Yep, he said. We all three laughed at the wonder of it. You were one hell of a swimmer, Mac said.

I thought dying people were supposed to be in hospitals but here he was in this hotel room, one shoe off, telling stories.

I sat on a corner of the bed across from the writer. We were about the same age. I was breaking up with the woman I'd come with, quitting my job at the bookstore, trying to figure out how to live the way writers lived. If they lived.

Of that small company in the motel room—fated couples, writers doomed to middling success or none, suicides quick and slow—that he would be the one to take his last drink that summer. To live another ten years and fulfill the sad and beautiful promise of his work.

We left cousin Grover sitting on the bed. Like a migrant worker or an old fighter, waiting for a job or a bout in another town.

Mac and I closed the door behind us. The hallway was dark and smelled of dust and old hotels in summer. And that's all there was to it.

Except for the missing sock and shoe. And the view of the Pacific.

return of the dead log people

*—H.J. Andrews Experimental Forest,
   Log Decomposition Site*

thank you for your participation in the blue river bone
orchard's bicentennial morticultural conference: the role of
the dead in carbon budgeting

but don't think of it as over and done. we are everything still
to come

all the indignities you're afraid will happen to you are
happening here and now

all the mortal invasions you keep from the house of the living
from the porches of your ears, the eaves of your seeing
openings you don't want eaten into, eggs hatching
little ideas in your brain, microbes growing furry unspeakable
words on your tongue, the dark juices of your heart
gone to feed the living

upstart salal and Oregon grape
sapling of cedar & hemlock and fir
thriving in our cold wet breath

perceived by you as a chill in the air and in those green bones
with which you thought you'd walked away unchanged

in your breath now
our breath
and in our breath our words

which you will know as a new stiffness in your limbs
a whisper in your many-branched veins and at last by

silence and time
and your dust will fall on us as gently as the rain
and we will take you in as easily as you
breathed our air today

thank you again
we look forward to your input.

Dear Sue

After a thousand miles, multiple stops and barely-made connections, having seen what's happening to friends and family and the planet, I knew our chances of meeting were bound to be slim.

A single misplaced digit of the dozens I dialed. Blaming my former self. He always got things wrong.

We have pushed the odds and now the odds are pushing back.

What are they, do you think, of walking down Third Street from my son's office and meeting an old friend from home and a few minutes later meeting my other son on the East Bay train.

Weird is the old word for fate. Our odds. The chance of one cell and not another. The interplay of time and probability. A synapse fails to connect. A finger hits a wrong key.

The son in the office helps people like we're getting to be when the care system breaks down as it does every day.

The son on the train was coming from another office where he tries to not let the air contain particles that might kill you and a statistically significant number of others.

We have replaced and improved the messy and unprofitable way the earth does business with volatile carbon compounds and electronic waves so instead of a ruin like me getting bone cancer my young niece Lizzy gets it and your sweet Malcolm, the voice of the Salmon River, in his throat when all he wants is to talk and tell stories.

We have crowded the angels and demons into a corner. Any little act may lead to a miracle of joy or sorrow.

Having multiplied the number of things we've figured out how to control by the number of ways we can be wrong, nothing is made better but we are addicted to contingency.

Missing you in the city in winter, I'll try to see you upriver in spring.

    Where the fruit trees will be blooming, unless we've changed the season by the number of days or degrees we forgot to subtract from the number we were counting on.

    After all these years of working to inhabit a little portion of the earth we find its great cycles so distorted by human investment in instability we are like our younger selves again: incendiary, running the streets, riding our luck.

Sorry I missed you.

    Jerry

The Monument

Have you been to the Big Island before? The woman who comes to clean the little pool behind our Kona rental wants to know. Third time, I say. We have friends in Volcano. Like we're almost native. We saw spinner dolphins this morning. *Nai'a*.

There's a tour boat, she says. Goes to Kealakekua Bay—lots of dolphins. And the Captain Cook monument. Wait. She goes to her car and comes back with brochures. I tell her we're planning to drive there tomorrow. Be sure and mention my name, she says. Susie.

As if already written, the English ships coming upon these islands. Returning in the season of *Lono*, a time of forbearance.

Next morning we follow a narrow road winding through jungle and coffee farms down to the coast. At a corner of the bay an old concrete boat launch, a dirt parking lot, a dozen cars. Picnic tables under trees, locals hanging out. Island music. Island business. Courtship. Child care. Kayak rentals.

The road follows the edge of the bay for a quarter mile, ends at a little park. Old concrete block yellow-painted restrooms. A narrow beach, kids surfing and socializing. A trail takes us away from the water toward an immense platform built of volcanic rock. *Heiau*. Where violators of *kapu* were punished. A sign says not to go there. On our way back the kids give us the teen-age secret look.

That these islands should be found by Polynesian navigators a thousand years ago. That they returned with everything necessary to their life and culture. Like an experiment of the gods.

If they can get it right anywhere, it will be here.

Down at the boat launch a young man is loading kayaks onto a truck. We discuss terms and availability. Shake hands. His name is Moki. We tell him we'll be right back, drive to the park again to change into our bathing suits.

When we get back there's a pair of blue and white cop cars in the parking lot. Uniforms standing around, two of them talking to Moki. This area was once sacred to Lono, reserved for priests and royalty. Now a historical and marine life conservation district. Sanctioned tour boats. Licensed kayak rentals only.

That the February winds would crack the *Resolution's* foremast. So the English return after violating every *kapu*. Build a storage shed on the *heiau*. Take its fence for firewood. The season of *Lono* being over.

At the edge of the parking lot Moki's girlfriend is sitting on a rock, her head in her hands. Jenny sits next to her. It's like this at home, she tells her. It's like this everywhere, I say. Another cop car arrives. Like *Hawaii Five-O*.

One of the cops comes over and stands beside us, writing in a notebook. I confess we're here to rent a kayak. Attempted tourism.

Across the bay, the *nai'a* are leaping from the water, spinning, throwing off showers of light. White foam splashing as they fall back into the green water. *Kealakekua*: Pathway of the Gods. On the other shore, on the beach ceded to the British by Hawaii's queen, the angular white phallus commemorating Captain James Cook.

A tow truck arrives to impound the truck and all the kayaks. Turns out they belong to Moki's uncle. Major loss of family income. Serious fines. The new *kapu*.

The cops are wrapping it up, looking the other way when a rented kayak comes back in. Jenny slips the girlfriend five Hamiltons and before you can say the name of the Hawaiian national fish we are out on the water in a yellow plastic kayak.

A couple of tour boats, maybe Susie's friends, are anchored near the monument. On the beach people walk around the stone obelisk. We begin to paddle toward it but there's a stiff breeze. A tourist helicopter is dipping and churning the air above us, making it impossible to navigate our big bathtub toy.

Other couples glide past us, paddling in harmony. We splash along till we're exhausted, stop below the cliffs. Caves up there, the bones of old Hawaiian kings and queens. Big hole in the cliff where Cook demonstrated the power of his cannon. This is as far as we're going.

A chisel and other tools were stolen from the *Resolution*. Cook, leading a company of marines, seized a respected elder and attempted to take him back to his ship as a hostage. Teach the natives about power and private property. In the violence that followed Cook died in the surf, run through by a long knife acquired in trade the day before.

The afternoon breeze brings the sound of sirens, Moki and the kayaks on the way to judgment. The helicopter finally swoops away and one by one the tour boats depart. The *nai'a* are swimming all around us now, dozens of them. We're supposed to stay fifty yards away but can't move our kayak fast enough.

Our snorkeling is even clumsier. Getting back into the kayak I tip Jenny into the water, barely save her sunglasses. Dolphins all around us now, their hoarse breath like laughter.

Stay back, I tell them. We could be arrested. They laugh.

Let's try this, the gods said.

> *Boys and girls at the water's edge*
> *   and hanging by the parking lot.*
> *On the green water of Kealakekua*
> *   the nai'a spinning in showers of light.*

Shopping for the Revolution

– for Jdimytai Damour

It had been a long meeting, an agenda of a thousand winters. We had come to a crucial moment in the struggle. All the prognosticators said down. Things were finally going our way. The Order of our Congress declared: Go to Middle Earth and live among the lost and unbelieving. Shop.

After all the years underground it took a while to recognize where I was. In astonishment at the bright lights and seasonal music, in Harris' Department Store in San Bernardino, I was a kid out of school because it was almost Christmas. My mother took me with her when she went to work at Markell's Jewelers and all day I wandered with a few saved dollars in my pocket amid the crowds of shoppers and animated elves and angels in store windows and the many-colored lights and tall buildings full of everything on Earth for sale.

And when I as a child had chosen my gifts and brought them to the counter the saleswoman put my money and a sales slip in a canister that she inserted into a brass tube and when she closed its round door the cylinder and its contents were sucked up to the ceiling high above us where it joined other brass tubes connected to an office with windows that looked down on the great ceremonial hall and the hundreds and hundreds of people enacting the seasonal sacraments of human commerce.

Up in the office accountant seraphim opened the cylinders and counted the money and performed certain ritual incantations and then put paper and money back in the canister and down it came like the holy spirit in its bright brass tube and a bell dinged and the saleswoman opened another little round door and there was my receipt and some change.

This was in the time of America's brief holiday between the great war and the lesser wars that were to come and the atomic winters that came with them. There would be an attempted spring. A thawing of spirit, almost a summer. But the warming spell got translated into a hundred and eighty minus degrees of deniability so that things turned out even colder but with the added fervor and cruelty of humans when they know their crazy ideas are killing them but they don't care as long as quarterly projections are met. Heaven on Earth, they proclaimed. A season of giving.

Finally even hell froze over, like we always said it would when the revolution came. Thousands and thousands of us wakened from our sleeper cells to go shopping for the spiritual resistance. Not to save capitalism. Not to rescue materialism. The light of the underworld was all we were bringing—the subterranean sun that rises when we find or make or care for something and give it to another person. In every transaction a fiery certificate, letters burning with the red ink of the underworld.

♪

Standing at the counter like when I was a child I handed the young sales woman my selection. A silver ribbon. A green bough. A clear river. A home for the homeless. She rang it all up with the light of the gift in her eyes. She didn't notice the smoke still coming from my clothing. The strange words on my money.

The gift would stay with her and in every transaction of her day. I walked out the door feeling its value still in my pocket. As if my money had gone up the brass tube like a message to heaven from the underworld, only to fall back as a blessing like rain. Like fire. Like music that ascends the bright conduit of prayer and returns as a song for the overthrow of a world where everything is for sale.

Thank you, she said. Here is your change.

Unwrapping the Sun

Winter green huckleberry leaf. Winter black alder cone. Bare wet branch. Splashing rivulet. The light before the rain. Light when the rain has stopped. The sun magnified by distance. Always in our eyes. Floating on the hazy air. The never quite drying air. Making us light little suns indoors. Causing us to sing. Winter shining out of human mouths. Winter light in children's eyes. Seeing that the sun is a child. Cradled in green. Bundled in snow. Lullaby of overflow. Little fingers of frost. Counting those we've lost. Looked for in every spark. Felt in every part of us. Hope and fear spending the long night together. Giving one another gifts. Wrapped in rain. Cradled in fire. Inviting human hearts to burn.

V. KEEPING OUR DARKNESS

east bay dream with power lines

in the criss-crossed tangle of high-volt and telecom guy-wired poles upholding cross-arm and insulator carrying filament carrying copper carrying electron carrying power & message spun by dynamo spun by river and by fossil carbon our fear. loss of power. loss of connection. we put our faith in east bay dream authority

crowds of people shuffle in line in the open well-lit dmv office to register vehicle or get license to drive around in their white-line lives. kid getting learner's permit to get on urban streets to be mario andretti of the dream not nightmare of san pablo ave

o east bay corridor o metro bus o bart o store front store front o mini-mall and maxi-mall o streets of old el cerrito and mira vista and vanished little towns and stores o past time hardware o choy's wigs o hotsy totsy club o launderland of our hearts and urban arteries clogged in the afternoon commute to wherever home has moved to

in the transit station new schedules posted with new departures and arrivals interpolated between old lines announcing new dream train stops. *look, they've added two more*. signs that our conspiracy is working. they are smaller and fewer than the official stops but the important thing is we know they're there. you and me and the two other people waiting for our dream to arrive and take us some place

from the hills of kensington to the salt flats of richmond from lake merritt to berkeley pier o mercurial fish o power grid of unsustainable joy o adult video and toy o red onion o mallard club o end of line and cable o last phone booth o wave of emf o thrill passing through us o free wi fi o constant buzz o neuron o wayward cell o path of message hello now yes now o urban sky o undergrounding of backstreet lines of memory and short-cut down the alley to the dream now streaming without end

geology of the eastern sierra

rising from the valley floor up through foothills to peaks of ten and twelve thousand feet a tilted edge of granite 70 miles wide and 400 miles long shoving upward now for several hundred million years

& on the eastern side falling into the unfinished edge of history

a high desert plateau where the pacific plate continues to jam beneath north america and the heat of their engagement comes up as plutonic rock and gas and here and there a hot spring

we've been driving dirt roads along the upper owens river for more than an hour. the directions to hot springs a mystery to be followed till hope and understanding are lost. there's not a lot of room out here for hope and understanding. this has to be the way

on a low hill in the alkali distance a naked human form, then another. a side road takes us toward them across the caldera. *long valley* a couple of hundred square miles of sage and remnant debris from a cataclysmic eruption about three quarters of a million years ago

at the end of the road two parallel lines of large rocks, between them a raised path leading across the alkali and up to a round pool, a labor of many days

about twelve feet across and a couple of feet deep, walls of mortared rock, more days. two plastic water pipes, the hot splashing into the pool, cold running on the ground for now. three guys soaking and drinking beer. the oldest says, there's always room for more

it's windy and overcast. jenny says she's chilled so she and the dog go off botanizing in the sage brush. I almost go with them. we came up from sea level yesterday. a couple of hours ago we were at 9,000 feet, on the granite peaks off to the west. first week of june, still snow up there. overlooking the valley we tried to imagine all that earth and rock, every living thing that was here, now this vast depression we're in, all of it blown into the sky

you realize, says the oldest guy, you're taking your life in your hands

one foot in the pool, the water is very hot, I say I think it'll be worth it. one of the guys is wearing a strange khaki hood, like something left behind by a long-ago desert army. now I see that he and the third guy are nearly as old as the guy who invited us in, who is almost as old as me

the sierra rises from the valley and then drops into this basin but we're a mile higher on this side. the earth underneath us still rising. the whole chunk of granite from whitney to lassen still being shoved upward and westward, the fire down there still burning

we talk about history. they were students around the time I taught college. late sixties. the draft, before the lottery. if you lost your 2-S deferment it was canada, self-destruction, or the national guard. they had protested the war, resisted the draft, ended up in vietnam. now here

I tell them I left the midwest university where I was teaching because I couldn't keep you guys out of the war. the university being part of it. students' lives depending on some dean or what grade they got in english. buildings burning, teachers and students being clubbed and tear gassed. no place for learning unless you wanted it the hard way

a hundred and fifty cubic miles of molten rock and ash went up, dust raining down as far as kansas. then we were driving across it, running back west. speedometer pegged at eighty-five, corn fields and ditch weed flashing by along the interstate

the guy with the hood is getting out of the pool. I tried to join the national guard, he says. today that would get you afghanistan, says the third guy. but the guard wouldn't let me in, taking his hood off now, dressing quickly in the wind

you were lucky, says the guy almost as old as me. the guard would've sent you to kent state to shoot other students

they ask where we're from. the redwoods, I say. the foggy coast. we come out here to put the fire back in our bones. but then I have to get out of the steaming water. I'm still recovering from yesterday's hot spring. I towel off hurriedly, thank them for their hospitality

the third guy drains his beer. we changed the world, he says

yeah, I say. maybe we did. looking east across the valley now, as if there might be the proof of it. as if they were my students now grown old and there was our lesson, clouds of white dust blowing across the eastern horizon, ancient blue mountains in the hazy beyond

the oldest guy asks the one with the hood if he's coming to

cut firewood tomorrow. I imagine it's what they do for summer money, work on the ski slopes in winter. we live up there, one of them had said, pointing to the volcano where we were this morning

the guy with the hood says a storm is coming, not a good day to be in the woods. then he says, I don't know if anything changed

this valley floor has risen three times from beneath an ocean, most recently a hundred million years ago. they can cut wood another day

I say I don't know either. maybe it's just taking longer than we thought

    almost summer
        change bubbling up from below
            there's always room for more

A Walk with Federico García Lorca

—Granada / Ronda / Cueva de la Pileta

Punctually, a las quatro y media in the afternoon, our guiding spirit arrives with a key. She opens the front door of the house and invites us in: a handful of elderly poets, lovers and teachers of his poems. It's Miercoles, admission is free.

He's not in the sala, not seated at the gleaming black piano. We find him in a little room upstairs, a child's room with blue curtains on the window. The bed neatly made, the narrow bed where he dreamed. The desk where he worked. At both ends of the desk little compartments where voices are still waiting to walk onstage.

To speak of love and death and transformation.

I'm not political, he said, when the Falangists took him from this house to which he never returned.

Out the window in the streets of Granada it's a week of elections and bullfights. The party of love and the party of death are making the usual promises. The party of transformation declares that it is changing. But even with loudspeakers it's impossible to hear them because the stone streets of Granada are so loudly proclaiming his poems. In the Albaicín, at the Quatro Gatos Café, they serve them with coffee and bread and jazz.

Out the blue-curtained window he could see mountains. Sierra capped with snow, even in May. Now we see the apartments and offices of fascist modernismo, much like at home.

Take him with you, says the spirit. Get him out of this little room. This child's bed. That bed of Spanish earth. Don't look for him here. Give up digging in the fields outside of town.

Walk with him through the streets of Granada, among the lovers and poets and painters. Arm in arm with his brash Dalí, his petulant Buñuel. His love that is not political.

Walk beside his river, el Darro, losing and finding itself between the hilltop towers of Alhambra and the steep winding lanes of Albaicín. Follow it in the pools and gardens of the palace, repeating all the names of God. In the fountains in the plazas of the neighborhoods, singing the life of the people. The water is not political.

Let the cobbles move beneath your feet, streets of stone flowing down to the river. Flowing in the voices of the bars and cafes, water over stone. Voices of Greek and Roman. Berber and Moor. Jew and Gypsy. Flowing in the streets and walls, voices of Iberian stone.

Walk with him downtown among the stone walls of Al-Andalus. The still living walls of mural and mosaic, the graffiti and poster of the moment. Lorca's children living on the streets of Granada. Some in masks, indignados. Some in gypsy leather, not political.

In cafes the three big parties and their candidates for EU fill the tv commercials but no one pays attention because the news is all about the three toreros gored by bulls this week. Every afternoon on the tv in the cafes, blood gushing from the thigh of España. The people can't stop watching.

Blood flows like conversation in the cafes. Like water in el Darro. Like snow melt from the Sierra flowing from the mountain towns, the white towns where he once walked and is now walking the roads from town to town. The dry earth beneath our feet, like the earth in the bull ring thirsting for blood. The poet gets down from his fine Spanish horse and on foot he faces the black animal of his dreams. He turns his back to the bull of España. Walks away. The crowd cheered him then.

But he turned around. Back to his father's house, patrimony of sugar and privilege. Bankers and generals. His mother's house of sin and punishment. Priests and judges. He should have gone to Paris with the painter and maker of movies. Instead he stayed and became what the fascists could not forgive.

They said he was political.

Walk with him down to the ancient bath, domed and subterranean. Bathe with the dead Romans, then the Nazrim. Al Andalus, 700 years of water over stone speaking of love and death and transformation. Till Christian armies take Granada 1492, banish Moor and Jew and Gypsy and use the confiscated wealth to underwrite the Inquisition and transport it with Cristobal Colón to the New World.

Walk with him, says the spirit of the buried past. She opens the door and we are welcomed by the thousands of missing and disappeared. Bones piled on bones, as deep as song.

The spirit gives us flashlights and we descend into the limestone womb of Iberia, into the cave where for 25,000 years artists conjured bull and horse and boar. Deep within stone making images by fire. Making songs to protect and nurture our darkness. To keep our darkness alive.

Walk with him, ancient boy, child of Europa. Travel into the future over the melting ice caps. Wander the roads of the New World with the children of Walt Whitman. Hang out in the bars of North Beach with his faithful correspondent Jack Spicer. With all the dead lovers and teachers of his poetry. The ones who will make the poem we need now.

Life isn't political.

To deny it is political.

Gacela for the New World

Tell them I'm not dead.

Someone miscounted the tickets.
Go see for yourself. A cemetery of dictators.

The puppet outlives the hand.

My moon is still faithful.
My tears in every rain.

But everything is transformed.

Earth and blood
outlive the banks and churches.

A cemetery of messages.

So yes, tell them yes, I died
but only because only the dead

can make the song you need.

The rain has turned his face.
The moon not the goddess she was.

Only the song does not change.

Look for me in a basement cafe
seated at the piano, singing to the fire.

Gypsy shadows on the walls.

I Dreamed I Was at a Watershed Meeting

Out of the woods. A lost human. Another. They call a meeting. They have a plan. Back, they say. To the woods. Stabilize stream bank. Plant tree. Sing water song. Make forest music. They hear a voice. Listen, it says.

The water and tree people, naiad and dryad, are once again calling the watershed to order. Convening a hearing. Calling for salmon. The meeting can't begin without salmon. Sing for rain, someone says. Everyone sings and it rains and sure enough the salmon arrive. First one, then a pair, then more, till there is a quorum. Now things can get started.

A bear gets up and wants to know if there are any changes to the agenda. A mountain lion moves to approve. It's unanimous. There is only one item: the fate of the earth. Everybody gets a voice. Someone wants to throw out the humans, but they get to stay. Humans can sing. Humans can dream.

Let the meeting go on.

Infrastructure

"How did it get like this?"

We're crossing an old footbridge, posts and rails piled thick with moss. Rotten planks under our feet. A rivulet spills beneath us, sparkling in the forest shade. Huge ferns. Skunk cabbage with enormous leaves, delicate water cress and tiny club moss.

"I don't know," I say. We come up here every year or two, hike this section of coastal trail to a picnic spot high above a wild beach. It doesn't look like any maintenance has been done since our last visit. The trail is littered with down branches. Every half mile or so another bridge with a rail fallen off, a broken plank where someone's foot went through.

I ask, "When do you think they were built?" Jenny worked remodel carpentry for twenty years and has a good eye for how things fall apart. This trail became part of Redwood National Park in the 1980s, but it's older than that. She thinks probably the '60s.

The trail follows an old logging road along the creek. A two-foot-wide spruce now rises from the middle of it. Another forest, high above us, grows from its moss-covered branches. Down the slope, enormous amputated redwood stumps. A bog of skunk cabbage, their stinky flowers bloomed and gone.

Repairing houses was also my livelihood for a couple of decades. I've thought of going back to it since the state cut my teaching job, but I'm falling apart myself. And there's not a lot of work out there. Jenny and her partner Mike haven't had a job in weeks. Today is Labor Day. I have an answer to her question. "Ronald Reagan."

The topsoil that sustains this forest is only a few inches deep. The trail is knobby and gnarled with shallow roots. We have to watch our step. "You mean when he was president?"

The trail dips down to a mushy boardwalk over a shallow feeder stream. Alders, some of the biggest I've seen, with huge branches broken off, new sprouts growing out of rotten trunks. The ground is a compost of their leaves, the air rich and sour with decay. Here and there a redwood, cedar, hemlock. "No. Earlier. When California elected him governor."

Jenny was on the streets of Berkeley when he sent in the CHP with shotguns. "Ah ha," she says slowly.

Ronny Ray Gun. B-actor able to believe his bad script, genial huckster for the screw-the-future gang. At war with their own young, with their own nature. The corporate warfare state reclaiming its hegemony after the '60s. Like 1660, the English monarchy back in power after only twenty years. Restoration, they called it. Killing the king wasn't enough.

We come to a recently rebuilt bridge. Jump up and down on the fat new cedar planks. Remnants of the old bridge thrown aside, decaying back into the forest. It's not over yet.

Our revolution came completely around. Whatever was dark and strange and unprofitable, what was natural in human nature, back beneath the surface. The perennial underground. Always emerging. Always over-turning.

Infrastructure. Is nature in human. Is human in nature with questions. "What are these?" Red huckleberry. Bitter. Spit it out. "What are those?" Deep reddish-brown, mucus-covered, rising out of a dead limb. "Jesus. I don't know." Orange mud oozing across the trail. "Iron," I say. "Ferrous sulfate," Jenny says.

On the bluffs far above the breakers and rocky coast we sit on a half-rotten bench eating our lunch. A stiff breeze, whitecaps on the hazy blue Pacific. This is as far as we're going. A young couple comes up the trail from the beach. "It's a good mile and a half," he says. "Steep." She says they love this trail. "It's great," she says. "Nobody comes here."

We remember when parks and schools and libraries were a source of public pride. We also remember testing atomic bombs and killing commies and spraying DDT on anything that moved. Equal measure of pride and fear and ignorance. Voting accordingly.

"Prop 13," I say, still working on Jenny's question. Cutting corporate taxes under the guise of helping elderly home-owners. Capital misdirecting the public mind. Private money corrupting public function. Hire cops not teachers. Build prisons instead of schools. Feudal estates instead of the commons.

Corruption. From the Latin: a bribe. In English: rot. Said of corrupted texts, corrupted meaning of words. Human institutions. Natural cycles altered. Natural wealth diverted. Decay spreading from the capitol building to this trail.

As we're finishing lunch a boy about ten comes up the path

that brought us here. Minutes later a couple in their thirties, breathing hard, struggling to keep up with him. The kid says, "We have to go all the way," takes off running down the trail to the beach. "Here we go," the mom says, laughing. Human families walking trails for ages.

As we're starting back I stop, pull a piece of leafy gray lettuce from a dead branch beside the trail. "Lobaria," I say. An ancient lichen. Jenny says, "Shouldn't it be green?" I brought some back from Oregon last year, left it on my desk for a month. "It changes color."

The trees have made a deal with the lobaria. The moss. Millions of years conspiring to rot together. Despite all we've cut down and wasted they'll be here long after we're gone. Our roots are shallow. Our heads a few feet above the ground.

What we are losing is not just a public amenity but the connection between human society and human nature. An agreement that we need to walk in the woods more than we need an empire.

On the way back we cross the new bridge again. Jenny loves the sound of our boots tramping on it. We go back and cross again. Even Rome one day replaced its last bridge.

A school or library is a bridge. To the outer world, the inner life. To the mysteries of death and renewal. The overturning. As the empire withdraws into corporate temples and shopping malls we are being abandoned. But loss is opportunity. Haven't we, in watersheds and neighborhoods and small towns, been building bridges with this day in mind? Falling apart as we are, haven't we become bridges ourselves? Aren't we about to find out what kind of weight we'll bear? Infrastructure.

In a mile or so we meet another couple. They're younger but weary and about to turn back. "No, you're almost there," says Jenny. "About three quarters," I have to add. "With steep switchbacks at the top." As they walk on, Jenny calls out, "It's worth it."

Our parks will be a wild commons again. Some trails will persist. *Facilities* will be a forgotten word. Not all the streams will have bridges. Some who use trails—who *inhabit* them—will also maintain them. The ones who like to go all the way. Local special districts, dedicated to community needs, may be the dominant mode of government. Parks and schools and libraries, wild and improvised, will rest on that deeper government we call culture.

We meet a young man about twenty, no one urging him on. We tell him he's about halfway there. "It's worth it," Jenny says. "She always says that," I say. We leave him standing in the path looking puzzled.

It's a long and uncertain way, the devolution from state and private property to bioregion and commons. It's happened before and will happen again. From human control system to natural process. To community and the wild interior. Trails to the places nobody goes.

> It won't be fast and it won't be easy
> but it will be worth it.

Small, Feathered Consolations

—for Scott

Two baby barn swallows wobbling on the wire outside my window.
It's their first day out of the nest.
They've been flying around after the parent birds,
awkward and unfamiliar with their wings.
Now and then, almost by accident, catching something to eat.
Now they're tired and want to be back in the nest.
When an older bird lands on the wire, they beg for food.
It flies away. Big mouths, pale fluff, scared and hungry.
A few days from now they'll be soaring over the garden,
hard to tell which are the older birds, which are the young.
It happens that fast.
In a few weeks they'll be gone. Some will be back next year,
some won't. Not all of us will be here to meet them.
Life seems designed to break us open.
With beauty, fear, joy and grief, a thousand ways.
Then it sends us out into nothing but faith and air.
This earth is a nest of broken shells.

To a Northern Spotted Owl

from the meadow
a dark shape
soundless
rises into the
douglas fir
beside my tent

the branch
bends
with her weight

last night
around the fire
naturalists
& nature-writers
doing owl calls

I try the basic
five-hoot greeting

she turns her head
a fraction
of how far it
could turn
regards me
opens her
wings
glides
one tree over
to an empty campsite

white-dappled
woods-dark

feathers upturned
at the tips for
silence

her temperature
the owl-man said
depends on
where she is
in the canopy

she wears the forest

warm and dry
in the tree-top

cool and wet
down here
where she hunts

she leaves her perch
swoops
onto the meadow
strikes
rises with
empty talons
returns to the
forest edge

besides mice &
voles & canopy
she requires a
new cavity
in an old tree

every year—
baby owls
like humans
leave a
big mess

what she gets
is industry
talking higher
rates of rotation
lower percentages
of retention
with buffer zones
& off-season
campgrounds

exile in our
own land

when winter
comes colder
& summers
broiling hot

we'll all wish
we had a
forest to wear

Breitenbush, Oregon

VI. LEAVING THE LIGHTS ON

Exhibit Ahead

> *The trees bring forth sweet Extacy*
> *To all who in the desart roam*
>   —William Blake, "The Mental Traveller"

Witness: Signs and wonders in the California desert. Consumers and marketers, seekers and spiritual providers, come here to save one another. Build homes remote from one another. Install alarms. Sell stuff. Buy stuff. Join churches. Multiple denominations wandering the greasewood and ephedra in the days before the holy rites of spring.

Country Gospel. Taco Bell. Freedom Baptist. Walmart. Nueva Vida. Home Depot. True Vine Fellowship. Faith in the Word.

Hi-Desert Star covers high school baseball, church news, obits, drug busts, DUIs, and break-ins. Victims and perps wandering the desert in search of one another. Retiree and service worker. Teen-ager and predatory tweaker. Neighbor and neighbor. Everything out here has been stolen at least once. Either from here or from somewhere else and brought here to be stolen again.

Yard sale art. Buildable acre. '93 Hyundai. Lawn furniture. Water.

The long ago far apart desert towns now one LA space colony half a mile wide and as far out the interstate as anyone can see or imagine. Remnants of early desert travel here and there. Curios. Dates. Live Reptiles. The old vacancies now continuous corporate western panorama. Rite Aid. Burger King. National Park. Marine Corps Air Ground Combat Center. Auto Zone. The place has everything.

Boys in green uniforms. Fence lizards. Rocks. Girls in brown uniforms. Joshua trees. Rocks.

Where the coyote and Cahuilla once roamed. Where then only missionaries, desert rats, a few boy scouts disturbed the solitude. Now view-seeking SUVs on paved roads. Read sign. Stay on trail. Park in designated space.

Mini-van. RV. Station wagon. Camper. Coupe de Ville!

Fire and water over millions of years. Making granite, breaking it into huge weird boulders, decomposing into sand. Joshua tree and sand. Desert, they call it. Like another planet, they say. Location for '50s alien flick *The Thing*. Weird background space music still here: Oo-whoo, oo-whoo. Drives the locals crazy.

Now at Yucca Valley Cinema: Oz, The Great and Powerful. G.I. Joe: Retaliation. Olympus Has Fallen.

It went like this, says the *Star:* Officers arrived after neighbors reported gunshots. Burglar's ninth visit this month according to homeowner. Stolen items include lawn furniture, garden hose, plaster lawn statuette. In spite of motion detector, lights, alarm.

Alerted homeowner appeared at front door with shotgun, confronted burglar who fled wearing woman's dress and a mask made of half a pair of pants. Brandishing a samurai sword. Burglar ignored shotgun blast and call to surrender, ran into desert losing both shoes.

Barrel cactus. Cholla. Rock. Prickly pear. Joshua Tree. Rock.

Suspect later arrested at his home. Puncture wounds consistent with running shoeless through desert. Several stolen items recovered from suspect's permanent yard sale. Homeowner says: *He didn't get my gnomes.*

Stolen. Every last piece of it. Serrano. Chemehuevi. Cahuilla. Land. Water. Silence. Nothing out there, they said. Acorn. Prickly pear. Piñon. Palm oasis. Desert, they called it.

Turn off the highway. Past the casino. Beyond the park. The signs. Where nature trail ends and nature begins. Wind in the piñon. Granite decomposing. Empire crumbling from the outside in.

Falling water table. Draining spirit. Lifelong tourists. Stranded souls. Church Of The End Of The World. Turn Here.

Joshua Tree, CA

Understanding Capitalism

—after re-reading Philip Levine

He picked us up out on 395, me and a friend hitchhiking at the edge of town, gave us a ride to Riverside. Along the way he asked if one of us wanted a job. Before Gary could answer I said, Sure.

I was fifteen and wanted money. I'd had some jobs that summer, but with unexpected costs. Driving tractor and disc over forty blackened acres, not wearing a hat, got a second-degree sunburn and my first doctor bill. Picking onions, clipping top and root, two five-gallon buckets to a bag, six cents a bag, enough to pay the doctor to sew up my left index finger.

The guy said his name was Morgan. He had a charcoal factory out in Railroad Canyon. Asked if I had a car. Sure, I said again.

I'd bought a '29 Ford for 75 dollars, with enough left over for a learner's permit and a couple of tanks of gas. For the rest of that August, in the early dawn, I drove the Model A across the San Jacinto Valley, stopping at least once to fill the radiator. Ground fog. Blackbirds calling across the fields. Then up into the Temescals, miles of dirt road, rabbits and brush, and Mister Morgan's charcoal factory.

On a rise just beyond the house, under a flat tin roof, a maze of angle iron, sprockets and chains and rubber conveyor belts outlined against the inland California sky. Across the road a mountain of burnt peach pits, trucked in from Arizona, waiting to be shoveled. A long conveyor belt took them up and over the road, then dumped them into a machine that ground them into dust. The whole place was black with the dust. The sun unrelenting. By mid-morning my brains were frying inside my new straw hat.

Under the tin roof another machine mixed the ground-up peach pits with a clear silicate syrup and pooped the mixture out as tubular charcoal briquettes. At the foot of the machine, Mr. Morgan's son-in-law sat on a box and broke off short lengths of the black goo as it oozed out and put them on a conveyor belt. A few feet away Mr. Morgan's pregnant daughter stood beside the belt and placed the wet briquettes on wire drying racks. The daughter and her skinny young husband seemed to me like slaves.

Now my job was to shelve the racks of wet briquettes, empty the dried ones onto another belt that filled a hopper so when I pulled a lever the briquettes would tumble into one of the cardboard boxes I had stapled together. Then I'd staple it shut and load it into Mr. Morgan's pickup to take to Riverside where he sold them in supermarkets.

It was the middle of the '50s. Emigrants from Nebraska and Iowa were building patios and learning to barbecue. The tubular briquettes let air flow through so they burned fast. They were wildly popular. I was making a dollar-ten an hour.

The earth around the factory was scorched and windless. Anything metal was too hot to touch. The black dust everywhere. My mother laughed when I came home from work. You look like Al Jolson, she said.

It'll wash off, I said. It's a good job.

Except for one thing. Every afternoon, in the hottest hour of the day, the daughter and son-in-law would go next door where I'd see them sitting in lawn chairs under a big cottonwood while Mr. Morgan's wife brought cold refreshments from the house.

It was one of those afternoons. I was filling and stapling boxes. Dust everywhere, the sun hammering mercilessly on the tin roof. I must have left my body because I could see myself from far away. The dollar-ten was nothing. I was nothing. A slave.

But I could quit. I could wash my face and learn to understand my condition. Wages. Privilege. Ownership of the means of production. I'd never heard of Karl Marx, but beneath the sweat and grime, burned into memory:

>The boss and the boss's family
>eating ice cream
>in the shade of the only tree for miles.

The Wall

We each of us took away some memorial of the place and reached the ship a little before dinner.
        —Andrew Bloxam

A palm grove and a spring. A shoulder of coral sand and black lava half embracing Honaunau Bay. On the landward side, from bay to ocean, a great stone wall separates us from the rest of the national park. We're in a *pu'ohonua*, the brochure says. A place of refuge.

Walking among widely spaced palms, Jenny and I follow a self-guided tour, at the end realize we've done it backward. Other clueless visitors follow us, out the opening in the wall where we were supposed to come in. Now we're on sacred ground, where Hawaii's royalty lived. Their houses are gone but the *heiau* where their bones were laid has been restored. Large wooden gods stand beside it, fierce visages looking out at the bay. We look around, walk back toward the wall.

Stones of all sizes, some weighing tons, shaped and set without mortar half a millennium ago. Ten feet high, nearly twice that thick in places. A thousand feet long, with this wide entry near one end. It was always open. You could walk in from the south along the beach. Or swim the mile across the bay. The wall is meant to let us in.

Like the gods facing the bay, the wall means *kapu*. That which is forbidden. The power we call law. Governing everything from marriage to planting to the food you ate, enforced by a hierarchy of nobility and priests. Breaking *kapu* could cost your life.

The opening in the wall means something else: *Aloha*.

Charity. The power we call love. Greater than *kapu*. Breakers of *kapu*, even enemies of war, could not be pursued beyond this opening. All you had to do was get here.

The English brought their own great powers. The book of love they preached and the book of law they lived by. Christian zeal and gunpowder. Half a century after Captain Cook, the Hawaiian king and queen died of measles on a visit to London and when their bodies were returned by the Vancouver expedition it was easy to believe the gods had died with them.

The new queen, newly converted, said no more *kapu*. Women could eat bananas. People could love whom they chose. She invited the ship's crew to take souvenirs. Take wood from the *heiau*, she said. Make it into collection baskets.

We are visiting from another colony, more recent than this. We know *kapu*. We have felt the king's shadow fall on us. Or ours has touched the queen. We have been trespassers in the royal grounds. Stood at the water's edge, watching the green turtles, the *honu*. They are the embodiment of peace. Nearly hunted to extinction, the brochure says. Now a protected species.

The park has many *kapu*. No smoking. No beach chairs, no picnics or pets. No frisbee, no football. *No possessing, destroying, injuring, defacing, removing, digging, or disturbing a structure or its fixtures.* This is an agency of the same government whose navy bombs these islands and chases people off their own beaches. To save what we love we build walls without openings.

They let me in with my Golden Age card. Jenny paid with the credit we got here on. The indebtedness we can't leave home without. Never knowing what *kapu* we're breaking. The old warrant we forgot about. The fine print we swore we'd read. The algorithm that didn't like our faces. Those things have less power here.

The Hawaiian people did not abandon their gods. The ancient kings and queens. The land. They have not surrendered to museums, geothermal plants, telescopes, new missionaries and sugar barons. The *heiau* remains. The wall stands. The gate is still open.

In a cove at the edge of the bay the *honu* swim with effortless grace. The gods gaze outward protecting what is sacred.

> We walk back through the opening
> into the refuge we came here for.

Blue Star

      somewhere in the marrow of my bones
      a fire is turning darkness into light
      whose speed when expressed as distance
      in miles per second times seconds per year
      amounts to 5.87 trillion multiplied
      by today's three score and ten
      placing me in the vicinity of zeta leporis
      a younger, brighter and bluer sun
      whose light on the day I first
      opened my eyes on earth arrived this
      morning in my bones in the kitchen
      in the november dark when I flip
      the switch connected by copper
      wire to a gas-burning generator that
      turns the bones of life a million
      years ago into light so I can see to
      fill the kettle and turn the knob
      to again turn time's off-gassing into
      fire to boil water to make coffee
      to sip while I read the news that
      this may lead to my extinction

      and by the light of zeta leporis
      I see my grandfather en la cocina
      in the morning dark an old man
      who grew up in the gold camps
      turn a knob and strike a match
      to make the bones of the earth
      boil water calling to my mother
      ¿café mijita? and in that old light
      I now see my granddaughters
      and their generation burning
      with the fire of their own stars

acting and speaking from their
offices and labs and the streets
to let us know that fracking
california's ancient past might not
be the smartest way to make coffee

I know it's hard to believe it took
five generations to figure this out
and a star's light to see it but it makes my
cup a little less bitter and brings my
bones that much closer to home.

Home Improvement

After much planning and discussion
we decided on the Bosch
64-pound electric. The Brute.
Like the sentimental song says:
breaking up is hard to do.

I picked it up from Don's Rent-All
early on Saturday morning.
Jenny did most of the jack-hammering.
I'm more of a bar and sledge guy.
So when I stop, the tool stops.

For almost a decade we had talked about
what to do with the back-entry sidewalk
poured by a previous owner
who liked to get drunk and mix cement.
During several of these episodes
he had poured three stretches of sidewalk
against a footing and on top of a slab—
all at conflicting angles and grades.

Mostly in our little differences
Jenny and I don't get out the Redi-Mix.
In the years we did, our arguments hardened
till we finally had to get counseling.
We would haul our slab of concrete
down to Harry's office on Third Street
where we hammered on it for more than a year.
Harry was a neo-Jungian. Our broken chunks
were nothing like those blocks of stone
Jung built his grail knight's castle with.
But we'd both worked construction.
With a little help we could take it from there.

Now the way is clear. Once the wood chips are down
we'll be able to walk from the back gate to our back door.
No stepping in puddles, no stubbed toes in the night.

Thanks, Don. Thank you, Harry.

A small improvement, I know, in these troubled days.
But it's one more human mistake made right
and that much less cement in the world.

The Way and the Light

It's 3 o'clock when I call. Friday. Labor Day weekend. Hoping maybe they'll get to it Tuesday. It won't be the first car I drove around with wires hanging out. A woman's voice answers.

"Hey," I say. "It's the Subaru headlight guy." She remembers.

Two repair bays and a tiny office on South Broadway. When I called them last year about changing a headlight bulb they were kind enough not to laugh. They did the work. A hundred bucks. To change a goddam light bulb. But I knew they'd earned it.

I had changed the first one. The driver's handbook advised I contact my dealer—but it gave directions. I can read. Unfasten and pull back rubber fender well cover. Turn steering wheel right or left. Fit your hand into a space you can see with only one near-sighted eye. Be careful not to touch bulb with your greasy human fingers. It took most of an afternoon.

"I got the old one out," I say over the phone. "But I can't get the new one in. I think I bent the spring clip." I can't even see the damn thing.

"Hang on," she says. She's looking at her schedule. "I've done the easy part," I say.

The other one burned out not long after. It's my own fault. I've been driving with my lights on since 9-11. But this sucker goes through low-beam bulbs like birthday candles. The mechanic took out half the engine compartment.

Afterward, as I was writing the hundred-dollar check, I asked the woman at the counter, "How many Subaru owners does it take to change a light bulb?" She looked at me. "None," I said. "They can't do it." That got half a smile.

I don't know why I tried to do it myself again. This entire civilization is designed to break down and be impossible to fix.

She finally comes back on the line: "How soon can you be here?"

Fifteen minutes later I'm at the counter. She comes in from the shop, wearing overalls same as the two guys. Straight shoulder-length hair, going gray. Observant eyes, the half smile. "Lou Ann," one of the guys hollers. It's almost closing time. "I'm going to do it myself," she calls back. She holds out her palms. "See? I have small hands."

There's a guy ahead of me waiting for an estimate on his Dodge pickup. A large man, he's helping his wife get her walker into the tiny employee bathroom. Then he sits in the plastic chair next to me. "We just came from St. Joe's," he says. "She's being treated for brain cancer." We talk about cars. I tell him about not being able to change a light bulb. He says both his sons own classics, a '67 El Camino and a '78 Firebird. When cars were still real.

His wife calls from the bathroom and he gets up to help her. When they come out he holds the door with one hand and supports her with the other. They're talking quietly and laughing. I can't imagine what's funny. They're still laughing when they maneuver the walker through the glass doors and out to the parking lot.

There are photos and paintings of old cars on every wall of the waiting room. Some of the cars are cherried out, bright color and gleaming chrome. Others rust away in barnyards and weed-grown fields.

She's done in less than half an hour. "Twenty bucks," she says. "That's not enough," I tell her. "It wasn't that hard," she says. "You already had it apart." She took out the battery, worked from above and below. I put a twenty in one of her small hands.

"I'll spend it on my vacation," she says. She's going to her sister's over in the valley for the weekend. I tell her again, twenty isn't enough. "I haven't had a vacation all year," she says. "It can't cost much to sit in the river."

Before I pull out I almost turn the headlight switch, then stop myself. After a few blocks on Broadway I turn them on.

> Blessed are those who fix the things we can't.
> Doubly blessed, who fix the things that nothing can fix.

looking upstream

at shallows moss-green
& rock-shadow green
& bubbling bright blue
foam-green & the deeper
darker current plunging
into the green of time

& an ouzel winging rock-
to-rock & I wonder if he
knows about the dam
a dozen miles downstream
the river made to work
for man

& at once I see
of course he knows
and so does the river
and so do I and
even when I'm gone

see the river in her
wild abandon
ouzel splashing
through rapids
creation
in its joyful dance

dams
and man
forgotten

& I take that river
with me when I go

Notes

These poems and stories arrived over the years in ways that seemed to require a name. A voice said, *Fugues*. Like in music? I wouldn't know where to begin. Or like, fugues employ counterpoised voices and themes? Maybe. Then I realized that the word meant *flight*.

Like what they used to call flights of Fancy? That winged horse nobody can ride? Or maybe just "going off," as they say in the psych ward? (Watch him. He's having one of his fugues.)

But I wanted to name them because it felt like they weren't coming from me. I was a dowser following a willow branch. A voice saying, *Dig Here*. (And then years of pick and shovel work.) Or like the Andalusian farmer who watched bats rising from a cave and one day decided to look for guano and instead found the animals of his ancestors' dreams. Or the guy in the telegraph office tapping out a message someone handed him, stopping to read it.

Dreams, Divinations, Dispatches. These notes identify some of the grounds of their emergence.

DESIGN One rainy spring I was a writer in residence at the H.J. Andrews Forest in Oregon, struggling with a one-act play about logging. Toward the end of my time there, poets Charles Goodrich and Clemens Starck drove up from the Willamette Valley, arriving like angels with take-out and the offer of a walk in the woods. Which turned out to be the real purpose of my residence there.

MAINTENANCE Alvord Desert, Oregon. The hot spring now has on-site managers and provides campsites, groceries, and restrooms. Call ahead. Arrangements for hot spring bathing are a foundation of human society. Like the geology beneath them, they are often renegotiated.

REFUGE The story of underground carpenters is from Dr. Tina Strobos of Amsterdam, who during the Nazi occupation sheltered many Jews in a specially constructed room in her home. When she died at the age of 95 her obituary (*New York Times* Feb. 29, 2012) included this story, which was shared with the homeless who had found shelter that winter with Occupy Eureka, Humboldt County Courthouse.

MY LIFE WITH MICKEY MOUSE This dream incorporates the City of Anaheim as it was in the year 1944, when my mother and sister and I lived for a time with my aunt. And again the year 1954, watching a giant crane pull up orange trees and pile them several stories high to be burned to make way for Disneyland. My great grandfather did have a gold mine in the San Bernardino Mountains but, except in this dream, I never saw a map.

THEY START ANOTHER GARDEN This fable came early in the "fugue" years, roughly the decade following our move from a house on the dunes facing the Pacific, across Humboldt Bay, to a valley of settled neighborhoods and farms. Less than ten miles, but moving is a recurring journey—you've arrived, you're home, yet awaken to a strange light every day. And in a corresponding otherworld, a psychic traveler moves with you. As with Jungian depth psychology, it brings into consciousness the roots and mortal attachments we carry from garden to garden.

PUTTING UP THE TENT Commissioned for the marriage of Marcia Brenta and Aryay Kalaki just as we were about to leave for a camping trip to Montana, where the poem then enacted itself. The poet just takes notes.

COMPOSITION FOR UPRIGHT PIANO & 1988 TOYOTA CAMRY   The Bob Dodge Memorial Cook-Off and Poker Game began as an annual Fourth of July celebration in the Klamath Mountains in the 1990s. Over the years new people arrived, others departed, and the event migrated to summer solstice at a sheep ranch in the Sonoma hills where a core group had homesteaded in the early 1970s. As with most tribal origin stories, there are several versions.

AFTER THE CRASH   The ritual import of fossil fuels has not been adequately recognized. Our last sacred fraction of oil reserves should be set aside for the preservation of the drag strip, the jalopy derby, racing in circles, and off-road human sacrifice.

NINE DAYS OUT   From the journal of a hot spring pilgrimage in the summer of 1997. Since the advent of Burning Man these sites have been heavily visited, many of them now fenced off by landowners.

The work of DeWayne Williams, aka Dooby the Guru of Gerlach, is posthumously documented and recognized in *Dooby Lane, Also Known As Guru Road*. Photographs by Peter Goin (https://www.petergoin.com/dooby-lane), Field Notes by Gary Snyder (Counterpoint: Berkeley, 2016).

SECOND LIVES   See Carol Sklenicka, *Raymond Carver: A Writer's Life* (New York, 2009). Richard Cortez Day, short story writer and teacher at Humboldt State University, brought this group from the Jambalaya Club to the Bella Vista to remind his former student, newly sober, that the love of writing was more important than the love of drinking. Dick Day was a superb story teller and teacher, and an unfailing mentor to the bar literati.

RETURN OF THE DEAD LOG PEOPLE   In 1985, at the H.J. Andrews Experimental Forest Log Decomposition Site, a variety of trees were felled and, to the disbelief of the faller, left on the forest floor to be studied for 200 years. *Rot: The Afterlife of Trees*, catalogs an exhibit of art, essays, and poetry at The Art Center, Corvallis, in 2016, some of it inspired by the decomp site.

THE MONUMENT   John Ledyard of Connecticut, whose company of marines was attached to Cook's expedition, provides the best account of the events leading to his death: *A Journal of Captain Cook's Last Voyage* (1783). See also Roger C. Smith, "We Shall Soon See the Consequences of Such Conduct: John Ledyard Revisited." [pdf. hawaii.edu, n.d.].

A popular snorkeling website briefly notes the history of illegal vendors, drug problems, and "uninviting vibe" at Napo'o po'o Pier, reassuring us that only state-licensed companies now rent kayaks for use on Kealakekua Bay.

The *nai'a* are traditionally regarded by Hawaiian fishermen as coequal beings.

SHOPPING FOR THE REVOLUTION   In 1927 the Harris brothers, Phillip, Arthur, and Herman, expanded from their little dry goods shop to a three-story "department" store that filled a city block of San Bernardino. Its wide sidewalks were crowded during Easter and Christmas holidays with families come to witness lavish automated window displays. The scale of the building, the grandeur of its entry arch, the columned high-ceilinged interior, all expressed a collective and quasi-religious devotion to shopping—much like a cathedral connects the devout to heaven.

"The Store For All The People," it advertised. That communal dimension of commerce diminished with the development of chain stores, malls, big boxes, and with e-commerce has disappeared into the soulless finger clicks of personal need.

Jdimytai Damour. Walmart worker trampled to death by shoppers on Black Friday, 2008. Walmart paid damages to Damour's family and others injured in the riot, but spent a million dollars and seven years fighting OSHA charges of endangering workers, eventually paying a fine of $7000. (Nathan Veshecco, "Jdimytai Damour: 10 Years Later." medium.com)

GEOLOGY OF THE EASTERN SIERRA The present generation of young people may find solace in learning that theirs is not the first to be sacrificed for the good of the few. Each generation, when it reacts to this betrayal with alienation and outrage, is given a label—lost, beat, hippy, punk, XYZ, or smeared with an old one—commie, faggot, witch. But the reality is that empire creates a continuous, self-renewing class of citizens living in a state of permanent resistance: *The Underground.*

A WALK WITH FEDERICO GARCÍA LORCA From a 2014 journey to Andalusia, Spain, that began with Granada and Lorca's childhood home, Huerte San Vicente. The visit coincided with the rise of Podemos and a rejection of the austerity regimes of global capitalism. It also saw the revival of the right-wing Falange and the uneasy ghosts of the Civil War.

Visit Café 4 Gatos. Placeta Cruz Verde, Albaicín, Granada. Desayunos & Tapas.

Cueva de la Pileta. Discovered in 1905 by Jose Bullón, a farmer hoping to find bat guano. The paintings on its walls are estimated to be 20,000 years old. Bullón's descendants continue to manage and guide tours of the cave.

Ronda. A mountain town distinguished by a deep chasm through its center and a bridge from which Falangists were thrown during the Civil War. Its hotels were once a favorite residence of writers, including Hemingway, Rilke, Orwell. Recommended: Hotel de la Poeta.

The White Towns. Los Pueblos Blancos, scattered through the mountain country of Andalusia, most within walking distance of another. Whitewashed and austere, situated on limestone mesas with narrow streets, they are intentionally difficult to access, reflecting their location on the ancient frontier between Arabic and Christian civilizations.

INFRASTRUCTURE   A park is not a forest. When the monarchs of Europe were deposed, the forests they had usurped (their parks) did not go back to the commons but to the state. When the patrician Teddy Roosevelt made a claim for federal jurisdiction over western lands (using federal troops against self-declared lords of poaching and grazing) it was thought it would save them. It now appears that a park must be either trampled to death or managed to death. Forests have never ceded their right of self-government, and they should be treated accordingly by those who know and respect their interests. (See Karl Marx, "Debates on the Laws of the Theft of Wood," Rheinische Zeitung, 1842, affirming people's historic stewardship of the forest.)

TO A NORTHERN SPOTTED OWL   Since this 2010 sighting the NSO has been threatened by the Barred Owl, which competes aggressively for food and territory as it expands its range westward. US Fish & Wildlife allows timber companies who shoot Barred Owls to then "take" the forest habitat of returning Spotted Owls because they're no longer indigenous.

THE WALL Andrew Bloxam was a naturalist aboard *The Blonde* on Vancouver's second expedition to the Pacific. Like the ship's officers, he returned to England with a number of Hawaiian sacred artifacts. The Queen's offer of wood may have been inspired by Cook's appropriation of another *heiau* fence 50 years earlier. Who would have thought they meant to burn it in their ship's stoves?

The only redeeming difference between colonialism and tourism is whether you pay too little or too much for what you bring home.

BLUE STAR Zeta Leporis. A bluish white dwarf star, roughly twice the mass of the sun and 15 times brighter, visible in the constellation Lepus (the rabbit) just south of Orion (the hunter). A very young star, possibly only 100 million years old. (*SolStation.com* 2008-06-26)

Porfirio Montijo was in his fifties when natural gas became readily available in southern California. He and my grandmother Guadalupe probably did not begin cooking with it before the 1920s. Southern California Gas had a surplus of locally produced gas until the post-war housing boom. Now all but 8% of its 11 million meters are supplied by imported gas, augmented since 2010 by the hydraulic fracture of shale deposits. ("Oil and Gas Production: History in California." California State Department of Conservation.)

Effective January 2020, the city of Berkeley banned the use of gas appliances in new homes and it's expected most municipalities will follow. As if Porfirio had lit a stove burner, its blue flame burned for 100 years, then went out.

HOME IMPROVEMENT Bollingen is the site near the upper lake of Zurich where Carl Jung in 1923 began to build a stone tower. Added to over the years, it became an outward expression of his investigation into the study of myth and archetype.

"Gradually, through my scientific work, I was able to put my fantasies and the contents of the unconscious on a solid footing. Words and paper, however, did not seem real enough to me; something more was needed.

"I had to achieve a kind of representation in stone of my innermost thoughts and of the knowledge I had acquired.

"Or, to put it another way, I had to make a confession of faith in stone."

                    (Carl Jung, *Memories, Dreams, Reflections*)

About the Author

Jerry Martien grew up in rural southern California, attended UC Riverside not long after it was built, went east to Rutgers University, then for several years taught English at Washington University in St. Louis. Becoming engaged in draft resistance more than academic life, in 1970 he and his family moved to Humboldt County where his anti-war work grew to include the defense of forests, rivers, and indigenous culture. He supported his writing and organizing with jobs as janitor, truck driver, bookstore clerk, doorman, agricultural worker, stream restorationist, and for 20 years a carpenter. He has taught writing in rural classrooms, high schools, and at Humboldt State University, edited and contributed to bioregional magazines, and has been a featured poet at readings for half a century.

Colophon

Letterpress printer, poet, editor, book artist and designer Kate Hitt established Many Names Press in 1993 for literary writers and artists to broadcast their exemplary works. Over the years, Many Names Press has printed and published such creatives as: fine artists Douglas McClellan, William S. Stipe and Andrea Rich; poets Louise Grassi Whitney, Eli Whitney, Barbara Leon, Hermie Medley, Maude Meehan, Amber Coverdale Sumrall and Patrice Vecchione; writers and poets Becky Taylor and Dena Taylor; novelist Leba Wine; and many others.

Kate was a long time resident of Santa Cruz county, and has returned to Humboldt County (where she once printed Jerry's chapbook, *Rocks Along the Coast* in 1984 on her first offset press). She holds a degree in Comparative Literature from the University of Virginia.

This book uses the fonts Arno (titling,) Goudy Old Style (body) and Goudy Trajan (cover). In 1915 American Type Founders acquired Goudy's fonts. He wrote, *I think of a letter and then mark around the thought. That is hardly real designing. It may be easy to think of one letter, but to think also of its twenty-five relations which with it form the alphabet and so to mark around them that they will combine in complete harmony and rhythm with each other and with all—that is the difficult thing, the successful doing of which constitutes design.*
—Frederic W. Goudy, *Elements of Lettering*, 1922.

www.ingramcontent.com/pod-product-compliance
Lightning Source LLC
Chambersburg PA
CBHW030333100526
44592CB00010B/682